# THE Wild LIFE OF Farm Animals

A **RUBES**® CARTOON BOOK   BY LEIGH RUBIN

**BOWTIE** PRESS®

LAGUNA HILLS, CALIFORNIA

*For Dr. Jyl, a friend to all creatures great and small.*

Nick Clemente, Special Consultant
Karla Austin, Project Manager
Ruth Strother, Editor-at-Large
Michelle Martinez, Editor
Michael Vincent Capozzi, Designer

Library of Congress Control Number:   2003102986

BowTie Press®
A Division of BowTie, Inc.
23172 Plaza Pointe Dr., Ste. 110
Laguna Hills, California 92653
949-855-8822

Printed and Bound in China
15 14 13 12 11 10 09 08         2 3 4 5 6 7 8 9 10

# Foreword

In 1945, George Orwell published his classic satire, Animal Farm, a tale in which a group of disgruntled pigs, horses, dogs, sheep, and other farm animals, no longer willing to remain subservient to their human master, throw off the shackles of oppression and take control of their own destinies.

Pretty heavy stuff.

But what if farm animals really were able to control their own lives? What sort of social hierarchy would they set up? Would they do a better job at running their own show or would they be just as goofy as the two-legged mammals who are currently in charge? And it makes you wonder (to paraphrase George Orwell), "If all animals are equally funny are some animals more equally funny than others?"

You decide.

Leigh Rubin

"Yes, Roger's here. Hold on, and I'll get him. He's just playing with the kids."

A scene from the sheep version of "Honey, I Shrunk the Kids"

"Just look at this floor. It's sparkling clean! You go back outside and track some mud in here this minute!"

"Whew! And they think *our* stalls are dirty!"

"Sid, Doris, I'd like you to meet Louise, my significant udder."

Few things are faster than roll call on a turkey ranch.

**Everywhere that Mary went, the lamb was sure to go.**

"And when you're done soakin' in that brine I want you to sit a spell in the smokehouse. You'll be cured in no time."

Common dinnertime conversation with the mule family.

"It appears that yet another fashion trend is destined to pass us by."

They knew their fate. There was no escape from the gleaming, razor-sharp clippers. It was to be a night of shear terror.

"The secret to my longevity? Well, my boy, it's really quite simple … I owe it all to unclean living!"

"I'm not exactly sure how it happened. I guess I was just plucking my eyebrows and sort of got carried away."

"As you requested sir—our finest cold duck."

"Oh, sure, sometimes I feel a little guilty but you have to admit, when it comes to seat covers, nothing beats genuine sheepskin."

**Where smoked ham comes from**

"Pushin' ain't gonna do us no good, Jed.
We'll have to use the kick-starter."

"And if you can't wait until morning, use this."

There was a strange chanting from the barn.
It was true—Old MacDonald had a cult.

Origin of steel wool

"It says here that pork bellies are up. Why, we could get a small fortune for your mother!"

"Stop it! Stop this horseplay immediately."

"Yes, dear, you can go outside and play, but watch where you step. Your father's been fertilizing again."

"Just how am I supposed to take a shower when all the stupid water keeps running right off my back?!"

"Gentlemen, as I'm sure you're all aware, this company has been experiencing a severe leadership crisis."

"Just what do you mean your father's never around to play catch with you?—That is your father!"

"Congratulations, Mr. Fryer. Your wife just gave birth to a dozen!"

"Hey, Pancho, when are you gonna quit workin' for the man and take control of your own destiny?"

Calves can be so cruel.

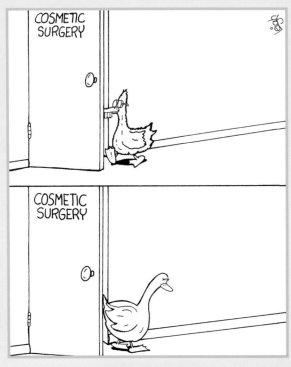

**A modern fairy tale**

"No, you may not wear lipstick! Number one, you're not old enough, and number two, you don't have any lips!"

"Whoa! What a filly! And she's completely bareback!"

"What nerve! Here they come again! What do you suppose the neighbors did for milk before we moved in?!"

"I see a very big future for you in textiles."

"Can you believe people actually go to fancy spas and pay hundreds of dollars to bathe in the same mud that we slop around in for free?!"

"Better come on in, Harriet. I think you've had enough sun for one day."

"Amazing! The kid's a natural. I've never seen any-one stick to a saddle quite like that!"

"Ya know, I really love this job!"

"That's your father up there. He graduated at the top of his flock."

**How farmers hit the snooze button
on their alarm clocks.**

Though the police put a tail on the suspect, they found it difficult to pin anything on him.

**The ugly truth about the ugly duckling.**

"Be a good little lamb and eat all of your grass so you'll grow up big and strong and become a seat cover like your father.

**Swine chivalry**

**Weather vain**

**Nighttime on the ranch**

**Squirt gun fights on the dairy farm.**

"Honestly, honey, I swear it's nothing!
She's just a decoy!"

"Well, I hope you're satisfied. Bo Peep was expecting us hours ago. Just once would it kill you to stop and ask for directions?!"

Things turn ugly and personal at the barnyard political debate.

"So, where are we off to tonight—dinner
and a movie?"

Horse thieves

Although a devout believer in reincarnation, Tom would be disappointed when all that he would return as were leftovers.

**The silence of the lambs**

"Boy, he must think we're pretty stupid to fall for that again."

Dinnertime conversation with the mustang family was limited at best.

**The dawn of latté**

**"What a waste of perfectly good food!"**

"The bad news is the high school dropout rate has reached an all time high. The good news is a lot less of us will be made into diplomas."

Though it wasn't a bad first attempt for a city boy, it was obvious to the ranch hands that Bobby's hog-tying technique needed a bit more work.

**On the scrambled egg ranch**

**Emotional saddle baggage**

**The dedication it takes to bring half-and-half to your local restaurant.**

**Old MacDonald *had* a farm.**

**Sheep gossip**

**The secret behind their "natural" curls.**

"Here's your three-piece chicken combo, sir."

**Pin the blame on the donkey**

**"For cryin' out loud . . . can't I even get any privacy in the nest room?"**

**Virgin wool**

"Did I ever tell you how I got this scar, son? It's
from an old college football injury. . ."

"Geez, had I known it would cost this much to fix my leg, I would have had the doctor take me out back and shoot me!"

"That's it! If the two of you can't get along, I'm going to confine the two of you to your veal pens!"

"And in conclusion, gentlemen, if we are to survive these uncertain financial times, the safest investment we can make is in ourselves!"

"Wow, according to a recent study you can live longer and healthier if you avoid becoming fried food."

"Y'all have got a lot of nerve complaining to me about being saddle sore."

"I'm sure you've all noticed by now that after the holiday there aren't many of us, pardon the expression, 'leftover.'"

"I don't understand why everybody is so excited about going on a stupid field trip. We spend our entire lives standing around in a field!"

Fed up and frustrated, the third little pig finally shows his freeloading friends that there's no such thing as a free lunch.

**Auto detailers of the Old West**

**The timing could not have been worse for an impromptu visit from the fourth little pig.**

**Origins of the devilled egg**

**Leigh Rubin** has been creating RUBES® cartoons for eighteen years. They now appear in hundreds of newspapers worldwide and grace millions of greeting cards, mugs, T-shirts, and dog bowls. Leigh is the author of ten books including *The Wild Life of Dogs*, *The Wild Life of Pets*, *The Wild Life of Cows*, *Rubes Bible Cartoons*, and the award-winning *Rubes-Then and Now*. Leigh is married and has three sons.

BowTie Press® is a division of BowTie, Inc., which is the world's largest publisher of pet magazines. For further information on your favorite pets, look for *Dog Fancy*, *Dogs USA*, *Cat Fancy*, *Cats USA*, *Horse Illustrated*, *Bird Talk*, *Reptiles*, *Aquarium Fish*, *Rabbits*, *Ferrets USA*, and many more.